C000124626

THE FLAYING OF MARSYAS

ANNEMARIE AUSTIN

THE
Flaying
OF
Marsyas

BLOODAXE BOOKS

Copyright © Annemarie Austin 1995

ISBN: 1 85224 328 7

First published 1995 by
Bloodaxe Books Ltd,
P.O. Box 1SN,
Newcastle upon Tyne NE99 1SN.

Bloodaxe Books Ltd acknowledges
the financial assistance of Northern Arts.

LEGAL NOTICE

All rights reserved. No part of this book may be
reproduced, stored in a retrieval system, or
transmitted in any form, or by any means, electronic,
mechanical, photocopying, recording or otherwise,
without prior written permission from Bloodaxe Books Ltd.

Requests to publish work from this book
must be sent to Bloodaxe Books Ltd.

Annemarie Austin has asserted her right under
Section 77 of the Copyright, Designs and Patents Act 1988
to be identified as the author of this work.

Cover printing by J. Thomson Colour Printers Ltd, Glasgow.

Printed in Great Britain by
Cromwell Press Ltd, Broughton Gifford, Melksham, Wiltshire.

Acknowledgements

Acknowledgements are due to the editors of the following publications in which some of these poems first appeared: *Ambit, Illuminations, Klaonica: poems for Bosnia* (Bloodaxe Books/ *The Independent*, 1993), *New Statesman and Society, New Welsh Review, Poetry and Audience, Poetry Durham, Poetry Now Headlines in Verse, Poetry Review, Smiths Knoll, The Rialto* and *Writing Women*.

Contents

I

The Flaying of Marsyas

Space hung down in the courtyard, and at the base of it
a young hawk floundered in a central flowerbed
with spread wings. It was a lord of flight
grounded on dusty earth among box hedges.
Its cry, sharp and urgent, ripped at the easy air
of this prison emptiness.
                  Inside, Titian's Marsyas
hung from his ribboned hooves on the castle wall
enduring the god's flensing knife at his shining side.
Silence. The adjectives drew back into the corners
of painting, room and courtyard, clearing the space
for the satyr who did what the poet has to do
and challenged heaven with his flight of song.

His pipes hung on the tree beside his heels, silent.
Silent his closed hung mouth. He did not recant.
Outside, the hawk raised its eyes to air and flew.

[Kroměříž, Czechoslovakia, 1991]

Of Formal Gardens

Interiors brought outdoors for clearer contemplation:
ceilings removed, we see into the rooms
we've walled with dense box hedges sheared
and manicured to coarse velvet; look from the parapet
of the top storey or from the upper terrace to
this horizontal vegetable life-size dolls' house.

Gaze from your sill down the verticals to see
the figure in the carpet magnified for study
in patterns of parterres. Stare at the bushes
turned like complex chair legs, crowned
with globes and cones as a newel post may be.
The sky, at a sharp angle, looks past your shoulder.

Our foot routes are legislated and curtailed,
laid out in fresh-raked gravel, straight as rulers
between shin-high box borders or viridian walls
that stretch beyond our hat crowns. At the ends
we find still further vistas painted to trick the eye
in niches of the garden stucco tipped towards us.

Interiors brought outdoors for clearer contemplation:
here is our gallery with works by the best masters;
they've pictured the perfect garden for us –
all geometry, and settled in that fulcrum moment
level between spring and summer. The dandelion
thrust through the gravel is easily stamped out.

Back and Forth

There is a forest and a white road and a field
where the glacial boulders stalled forever on
their southward courses and the Baronin walks alone

because they would not expect her to be there
who has all the manorhouse gardens at her disposal
with the lake and glasshouses and a pale-green temple

above the well from which a newborn baby's body was
fished only yesterday – but they have not told her
so that is not the reason why her lips are dry

why she has not touched them to either food or
liquid since the day broke in long flat rays
across that meadow where rocks ran aground

and even then she walked into the dense
extended shadows of the stones and out again
ceaselessly like a shuttle weaving the field

until it is completed then unpicking it once more
as Penelope did far south in Ithaca with suitors
waiting in her hall wide as the bathhouse/ballroom

here beside the manor's lake whose swans are
paralleling their own reflections back and forth
where she is not and the dead child is no longer.

Winter Without Me

Since I went away in the summer they have begun
their winter without me. I saw the crimson edge
of a leaf or two, but the roses raged still in
the markets and midges whirled within birch forests.

I have always shied away from a winter so far
north. The slant streets' cobbles shelled with ice
are terror for me, dogged by a phobia for skating and
the like. Imagine the slick surface of compacted snow!

So I left them and leave them to it as the nights
exhale, expand, lean on and shrink the daylight
up there, where an ice sheet's great boulders litter
the fields like pebbles raised on 'drink me' mixture.

And it happens without my contribution. The ice skin
spreads down the hill bearing grains of grit with it
over the broken pavements in the half-gloom of afternoon,
inside the Stygian grip of midnight well below zero.

And it happens without my knowledge. A death
that intimately diminishes me occurs out of sight,
up north, past the reach of my vision or inclination
who gave up my place there when the roses raged.

The Skeleton in the Cupboard...

is coiled in, wound like a snake in a spiral
of its spine, the knobbed beads of the vertebrae
balancing one on another, resting, embracing,
intimate as one woman's hands colliding quietly,
unsure which palm is touching, which is touched,
whether fingers of dexter or sinister take the lead.

It is one woman infinitely elongated in the dark
like the life of Woolf's Orlando stretched as a drumskin
on the centuries; this time she's skinless as a stone
or as strung stones in an endless necklace
looped carefully on itself in the cupboard they tried
to forget and papered over with a flower design.

Oh the long drip of phalanges into stalactites behind
the door, the bleaching of repeated knucklebones
where they hang then fold onto the floor; she grows
new small joints as years fade the covering paper,
fails to dwindle away, pressing those concentric rings
of her ribs into corners that remembering had left empty.

Here Are Candles

Here are candles for you, pale and tall.
I drop my three francs into the tin box on the wall
and take hold of the stem of one, balance
its hollow base on an iron spike and watch its flame
waver then flower straight up before this Virgin
dirtied by seven centuries of such thin smoke.

She shows as startled, and you must be too
at this tentative signal from a daughter
quiet on the subject through all the thirty years
since your dying with the priest's unction oil
on your forehead in that hospital side-ward
where you lay in wet sheets to slow the brain's bleeding.

And now suddenly – candles, candles in every church
on the Burgundy pilgrims' routes to Compostela;
an August week of white beeswax and tallow
in slender tapers and blunt nightlights – out of the blue,
out of the dark of this corner before any light
is struck in the face of the Virgin's astonishment.

Her head is close-wrapped, as yours was too –
in a caul of bandages on that damp mattress
where you died shrunken, waxen and unaware
that we were watching. Your eyes were open but
just as blank as hers now the painted pupils
have rubbed away with the rest of the polychrome.

The candles shape and colour her instead, make
something play upon the cheeks and lips that looks like
life. I cannot work this magic on your face.
The flames for you are tugged up into air
and lost above me in the chancel vaulting where
maybe you taste their fume and maybe nothing.

Victorian

Even rich faces make you think of the flour cut with
alum, used tea leaves dried again on a skillet
then sold at the kitchen door: adulteration
leeching colour from the cheeks, the peakiness
in every photograph; something unhealthy about
the stains under the eyes, the doughy flesh...

As here, where the Elder sisters are almost in
a fashion plate: hard to imagine a real occasion
that might combine the thick mantle worn by Louisine,
her muff like a cushion of fur and Annie's gown
that just grazes her shoulder bones, exposes
the tender elbows to our gaze and any draught...

That their faces expect, in the frozen pessimism
of the long exposure, the elderly disillusion
of children who know they are not meant to be heard,
whose withheld speech mounts up at the back
of their eyes, in the tight corners of those mouths
closed on watered butter, dust of pepper dust...

Dynastic

Joanna of Castile, 1479-1555
Margaret of Austria, 1480-1530
Catherine of Aragon, 1485-1536

1

You are two years old.
This is your wedding day.
In a great cathedral in a distant country
your uncle acts as proxy to repeat your marriage vows
per verba de futuro; and another child,
transported in his long clothes in a noblewoman's arms,
is bound to you as husband
sight unseen.

Now you are princess, duchess, *Madame le Reine* of France;
yours is the highest rank here in the castle;
someone is making you a little crown
just like a plaything but of serious gold
with real gems in its insets. You are cold
from their deference; no one may handle you,
and metalled fabric stands you stiff upright
and back from everybody in the rooms.

You learn the rule is 'to defend right and rank'
by 'honourable bearing', 'cold and self-assured'…
But what does it mean and where does it apply
when suddenly the bird springs up from the garden bush
and you try to toddle after in your jewels?

You cannot see the change to your body's nature:
that nested inside the child is a tiny woman
who is really the ring to enclose a king's
gold member; ring passed across an ocean
from one country to another in a giant's marriage;
ring whence the mongrel two-tongued children
must burst into the world and turn it
flat for themselves to lie on, all one throne…

18

You are the means, a flesh circle with the empty centre
through which the business of the dynasty is conducted,
the needle's eye whereby your family
may troop with all its goods to earthly heaven...
But this is secret from you, generally unsaid;
it shows as manufacture of bright cold gold instead.

2

The voyage out
                    from the nest, from first base,
                    into the eye of the wind;
                    from the rest of the same bone,
                    the known bodies, into empty space;
                    from the garden of the bird bush
                    into the sea's furrowed field...

You stand at the rail and pray mechanically –
'now and at the hour of our death, amen'; and then
blasphemously – 'if it be possible,
let this cup pass from me'. But the great vessel
of the sea is swilled by an unseen hand
and its waves lip against the rim of the horizon;
the cup is too big to pass away – you are in it
like a sop of bread and washed about
without any say in such a matter.

                    ...from hand to hand into nothing;
                    from the case of familiar rooms,
                    the original view from the window,
                    into a blur of sky like fainting;
                    from rugs and paintings, chairs,
                    into an endless blank...

Margaret, you believe you will die in this limbo
still unbedded. What is the use of that trained denial,
sacrifice to a distant father's will, unless
some end is reached, a real crown put on?
The deck lurches underneath you and the clouds
whirl round. You are sick at the very core
of your velvet metalled gown, your backbone
turned to a vial of troubled liquid. There's no land
in which to lay your virgin body down.

3

Each court is approximately the same
as every other court. But behind
a jewelled procession thin as cut-out paper:
a new and savage country with a different light
from yours, with house façades like steeples
and a people speaking with stuffed mouths –
the vowels spilling down their alien chins.

So he must be your home base
who was chosen husband almost at your birth:
Arthur or Henry, Charles or Juan, Philip or Philibert –
just names for the stable spot at the eye
of the whirling. You look at him again, again,
assessing his worth whom you must love
by prior arrangement...

And you fall, Joanna – as from a high tower
into a well – in another country where the population
splutter consonants towards you as they move
through soupy light that slops against
the stepped gable-ends of buildings.
He that is nicknamed 'Handsome' gives his hand
and you drop into the moistly echoing dark.

Lost utterly now, and blind to everything
except his touch, the glimmer of his face
at the end of the mole's tunnel, where he passes
with another lady in the circle of his arm.
Duty sits lightly on him, while your own
has merged into the marrow of your bones,
twisted within the heartstring strumming at your red centre.

4

Catherine, you are brought to bed again
of a dead child. This is not co-operating
with the dynastic plan whereby this man
spawns smaller replicas of himself
to fill the ever-diminishing-to-the-distance
thrones of an eternal kingdom.

Consider your sister. Her offspring will accept
a clutter of crowns in France, Portugal and Denmark,
in Hungary and the Empire. Ten years of effort
achieved this simple thing – live children
in the cradle and the crowds' acclaim
at trumpeters' loud announcements.

Instead you swim in the dim of a shrouded room
where waiting-women walk on tiptoe and restrain
their words. He visits you less each time,
the disappointed... all he has asked and you
have failed him, not doing what any washerwoman
can – springing red noisy babes again, again.

Though such a skivvy cannot bring
your blue-veined white skin to the task,
your jewels, your genealogy most of all.
It is a paradox: what makes you marriageable
must sap your strength for sweating labour –
those kissing cousins weighing down the tree.

5

Leftover life to be consumed in whatever way
it pleases you. You have shaken loose
from the dynastic process and swim on your own
at last in the cold indifferent sea. A widow
past your prime, a done-with person by and large,
locked in the pocket of your own obsession:
Joanna, in a place without windows, gazing at the beauty
of your Philip's embalmed face as he lies long dead;
Margaret, ordering the mausoleum where Philibert's
image and your own shall turn stone heads
to mix looks somewhere in the air between you;
and Catherine, grass widow, in those lonely manor houses,
refusing to surrender any name of queen or spouse...

It comes apart at a touch,
remaindering fragments
like a torn, illuminated
Book of Hours... a strip of knees
and spurs from a hunting expedition

...squares of so blue a distance
they draw the eyes to drown...
a platter or two from the banquet
where the cock stood up in the dish
and crowed (an attested miracle,
marginal here)...crowns on a journey
...so many disembodied lifted hands...

You tarnish slowly, growing a little shabbier
with each year away from married glory
when they polished you for appearances, those minions.
The ring thins on your finger, the slipper underneath
your heel, the bone inside its velvet sleeve.
With age you grow invisible to kings and popes
and princes; no longer ripe enough for
wedding-bed or childbed, withered, you are given
some space out of time for your own after all...
Soon you will stand in the midst of a ring
of birds as they fly up from their bushes
to circle above your head in the whirling sky.

II

The Sensible Child Meets Marsyas in the Wood

The Sensible Child wears a hat against the sun
and has practical walking shoes; her bag contains
some *sal volatile*, a flashlight and peppermints.

She is going through the wood, like Red Riding Hood,
for a purpose; so the half-man hung by his heels
is an obstacle to her, the clump of figures interruption.

What she sees is what there is – which is the sensible
rule – six persons and two dogs around the satyr
strung on his tree like a sack of flour being weighed.

The Sensible Child considers offering the peppermints
as precautionary declaration of conciliatory intent
from one in a dark wood alone and unprotected.

But none of them is looking at her, nobody seems concerned
at a stranger's arrival on this scene of obvious torture.
She lets her flashlight's beam play on their skins.

The god's is satin and the little dog's pelt gleams,
but blood streams down Marsyas's inverted torso
where the knives are lifting epidermis from his flesh.

The Sensible Child perceives he is already far beyond
such consolation as her smelling salts can proffer;
besides, the torch's probe disturbs his inward gaze.

She has no place where this judgement blocks the path
and the humus underfoot is fast puddling with blood
she must step over; the little dog laps there already.

There is a slice of air where his body swings out
from the ground of the picture – between the water bucket
and his yet unblemished side; she might slide through in that place.

The Sensible Child is off and away and running
to the pinprick of white at the end of the woodland dark.
When she gets home the police will hear about this business.

Babes

Down the gone wooden alleys that healed behind them
they went, seeing ways where no ways were,
making regularity because the trunks were straight
enough to do it, conjuring ranks from random...

only to look back on chaos, on routes that closed
with planting after all, on plaited walls of branches
and the light going always, withdrawing as leaves
thickened one on a hundred, a thousand on the rest;

into a deepening quiet in which beasts fell silent,
their cries bleaching out in the gathering blackness
like covered shoots or the blind fish of the sea bed
that shout to one another in unheard electricity...

The moon's eye could not find them from its
vertiginous height above the forest become all
dots and circles, spokes of branches about the axles
of the trunks, squat bushes as clots of leaves

through which the owl might be traced as a blown
white spark, the fox as a spent match whose last
glow lit its tail's tip, the wolf as darkness crawling
and smaller predators not at all in the undergrowth

below those moving cloud shadows that blotted
the night's spilled black ink out from its edges
or moonlight that turned the spread hands blue
in exposed rooms elsewhere – no flesh was detected here.

The Mermaid Examined

'In 1403, it is said, a mermaid was found in shallow water at Edam in Holland. She became accustomed to life on land but never learned to speak. She lived for some fifteen years after her capture, and was given Christian burial.'

She left an emptiness behind in the shallow water
like a print for trackers following – pockmark of air
they looked for after, once she was high and dry.

Because they had known mermaids – and she was wrong.
In low relief on the church's capitals were the siren
with two tails grinning into a mirror and another
sombre creature that suckled a famished lion.

But this one stank in a while and must be sluiced
with a pail of salt water once a day. Her strangeness
was blatant in the bruised and bleeding fins,
the mouth that gasped like a landed herring's.

And they thought in private of the words for their
secret parts, how the man's "snake" was answered
by the woman's pudendal "fish" underneath her homespun –
a covert conversation, best fitted for the dark.

Yet she in daylight twisted her swollen tail
within a thin drizzle of falling scales, out in the air
for all to see, like a woman whose leg-limbs
had withered away while her sex grew gigantic.

It was obscene as demons, worse than any carved
on the church misericords. They brought their dreams
out into waking to ask the dawn, 'How does
a mermaid make water? How does she shit?'

On holy and market days they peered through a window
into her room to find the answers. Though she leaned
inside a tent of homespun, they saw her fish
stir underneath the gown, line it with silver.

So the sprinkling with baptismal water was
attempted taming, the long hole in the churchyard
the safest place for one who would otherwise
swim into their heads for good and all and bring the chaos.

Mermadonna

1

Suckler: of the legged child in the crook of your elbow,
of the sinking lion on the church misericord whose
belly your thin arm circles like a bale of laundry.

Your milk is salt-tainted as if with tears and
the lion will twist away from it in a moment –
though the child, reared for sorrow, sucks on

and on. You give yourself endlessly through those globe
breasts as though your veins too ran milk and tears
or the pelican child took lifeblood from your dug.

The lion recognises the blood's salt-and-iron taste
rescuing him from ending inside a clear sea
that stings his eyes and tongue with other brine.

2

I abjure thee – like Satan and all his works –
who, in the guise of a children's tale, taught
longing and sacrifice and silence as desirous.

I asked for that story again and again, sucked
merwoman's tear stuff at your expansive breast
and let it flood my veins as well as words.

Like Scripture insinuated by repetition, its plot
encompassed me, became me, until I had a spine
made willowy with salt water of unrequited love,

feet that walked on the world cut by mermaid's
knife blades and a tongue kept back, withheld,
as I lived by looking and bided my time, bided my time.

Making Use

He enters her head through her eyes as though they were
tunnels, shafts into that brain-store, as though
they were twin drinking straws and himself the liquid
in the glass, standing where light slides through it.

He is lit for her attention, turns at her will on
the drum of the ground, in order that she may peruse
the angle of his cheekbone, how his head is carried
on its neckstem, how in speech his jaw drops down;

the slant of his spine, his colours, how his hands
rest at his sides, the rhythm of his walking –
as if somewhere there were a limp disguised...
She struggles to hold them all on call, in mind,

so that a tale may congeal about his figure,
attaching itself at those insignificant places –
beard hair, the web between the fingers, eyelash,
toenail – each one now sporting plumes of words

until he is cocooned in them and swallowed,
owned by her fiction, no longer his own man,
a jigsaw of his features stuck to the water-glass,
and all within – air damp after her drinking.

'Silos to Rent, Suitable for Growing Mushrooms'

After they took the grave goods from the tomb
it was like this; after they lifted from the Hunn
princess's breast the skeleton of the spread eagle
and cleared the gold plaques from her bones
one by one; after they moved her to the museum
so they might sift her left bed of black earth
for lost finger rings and verdigrised ear bobs:

an absence, a great "not" of unfilled socket,
the gape of a toothless mouth, a rifled nest,
discarded wrappings – anything purpose-built
whose motive has been snatched away and shed
like deciduous leaves when November comes...
the cold time of year, the Cold War god whose box
this was and from whence he was meant to spring

in winter, furling like dry ice from the opening
in the ground, hugging the ground, its contours,
riding its lifts and falls and long levels that
might as well be water, to a conflagration –
the god broken and made again a thousandfold,
risen and rising athwart the sky, ascended as
dust and vapour over a level-as-water earth...

Cruise gone, the god gone, worship departed with
the symptoms of winter, the personage of the monument
long trundled away – only the little organisms move
behind the steel doors thick as a double bed's width,
only the mushrooms rising in the dense dark
a thousandfold and more from their shelves of black earth:
smell of mould, pale underground plaques as grave goods.

Tomb

While life lasted I lived for others; now, after death,
I have not perished but in cold marble live for myself.
EPITAPH FROM A VENETIAN CHURCH

At last. To begin with, a long rest – calves, buttocks,
elbows cooled on the silken flesh of the stone,
soothed by its breath. No one summoning the day
by throwing back shutters on the canal's dazzle,
no one bringing a glass on a tray. The hurly burly's
done, the dark's drawn in to cover me with comfort.

What silence in which to try my voice's range
from bass up to falsetto, to scribble the darkness
with random phrases then run them together
in anarchistic song. The marble holds the notes
in a cold preserving vessel; they hang on it as
icicles and snow – so winter climbs the corners.

I roll my frozen body in these drifts with all
a bather's pleasure in the Lido's sunstruck waves.
Chill plays with my members, rings my limbs
with close frost bracelets then with zero sleeves.
Such a particular clothing, furnishing. Swathes
of spun blackness hang my tomb, my nest, this womb:

the matrix where I rebegin my living, grow
my self out of myself like a bulb in the dark
ground. My white finger shoots may grasp the air,
my flesh – no other ministration is required of me,
now dead and put away from the world's eyes
in a drawer of spices where I am kept alive.

Making a Boy

There are so many recipes. One woman, to begin with,
baked a gingerbread figure with modelled features
who came alive for her, as did Galatea after
Pygmalion's chisel had shaped her limbs from stone.

You can choose your material. From flowers such as
those that mixed to make Blodeuedd – oak and
broom and meadowsweet – to seasoned wood carved
to Pinocchio shape – the jointed puppet breathing.

And worse though still successful options. When
Frankenstein patched his guy together out of corpses
that could be galvanised to speech and walking,
he was glad, like Rabbi Loew with his mud golem.

So what shall I take to make my boy? Dark bogwater
for blood and the silken flesh of foreskins to hold it
in alongside the white birch bones slim and straight...
So far so good but nothing special. I await the spark.

An arc of them falling from the welder's torch to seal
that spirit inside the hollow tubes of silver which
could be limbs. The face is in low relief, metallic,
like those embossed on chalices for spacious drinking...

But I am alienated from this work of bronze and tin,
these games of gold and copper. Give me a little dough boy
after all, to sit in the palm of the hand at first
then swell from the yeast in him to lie along my arms.

Let him crust to a golden hardness of fist and elbow
in the oven. Let him scent the house through in all
the stages of his making till they guess in the street
at the boy's arrival. Let us eat him together again.

III

Goat Song

Tipped toward the light
that strikes his belly flush
so that the navel offers itself
as the lifted communion cup:

the goat drawn to the flame –
a moth to the candle –
to be held in the play of pain
by his ribbon-tied heels.

This is tragedy in the purest terms:
the perpendicular dive down
from the branches spread like arms
to the blood-puddled ground,

and the god turned artisan
at work with the flensing knife,
unpicking pelt and skin
beneath the sacrificial tree.

Stretched by gravity and agony,
his torso itself is a torch
consuming its very substance
to light the darkening forest

for a last suspended moment
while still the navel brims
and tilts toward us whole –
omphalos, about to be broken.

Blood

There is the blood.
          It falls.
                    It dribbles from the corner
of a mouth that is ten feet wide on the screen
above us. Death in the films does not happen
without blood any more.
                    It's spilt relentlessly,
as in the Hussite propaganda paintings where
Christ spurts his ichor out of side and palms
onto the lifted faces of the crowd below his cross.
Their veils and handkerchiefs are spattered,
held up towards him for the bloodmarks good as
Veronica's cloth.
                    Some cheer the baddie's bleeding
here in the cinema. It is assurance he does not feign
his hurt and is not sleeping. Death is certain, signed
by the blood-bag underneath his shirt, blood-capsule
in his ten-foot towering mouth.
                    And on those tongues
it was also surety: the wine-blood to re-animate
bread-body they had supped before, communion
'in both kinds'. No longer did they see the priests alone
guzzling that crimson liquor from the gallows tree.

Moonmen

Lorca's was a woodcutter –
all but his clown-white face –
and did the bidding of death
in the midnight forest,

lighting the route for bright knives
changing sheaths. There are other
moonmen: those who cannot sleep
when the moon is full,

and who wander seashores
or restricted floorboards,
troubled to their bones
by its unrelenting metal shining;

or astronauts in white –
all but their blank glass faces –
moving at moonrate and leaning down
to pick up dazzling rock.

Moonless

1 *Werewolf*

The silver bullet's long inertia has rotted the velvet
lining of its keeping case: the werewolf has grown
a hair or two over his fingernails, but that is all.

The window's blackness, blankness leans upon him
like a leaden plate. The need for moon to set him off
bleeds underneath his skin; he's haemophiliac with it.

Without it just a cypher, a formula face on the train
that enters tunnels no darker than the sky. His eye
expands to entertain this moonlessness with no prey.

2 *The Cow that Jumped*

'There's really no incentive. Oh it's well enough to leap the tree,
the hill, the mountain, but where's the truly cosmic act
to take this cow beyond the realm of fact and into legend?

The cat can fiddle all she likes – it makes no difference.
My feet spring from the ground, leaving behind the daisy
tussocks and the buttoning of purple thistle flowers,

but there's no target up above to aim for. The dog is sober
as a judge at the door of his kennel. The dishes stack
a low pile in the closet and spoons lie single in the drawer.

Oh the drawn-out days, the ennui for a cow with aspirations
past this meadow, this house, domestic animals and utensils.
Oh for a blue-white night and the thin bones of a bird!'

3 *Meeting*

The werewolf took the train beyond the city limits –
out to the Great Brine Lake where it endlessly lay and
manufactured salt crystals like compulsive knitting.

He waded morosely and at length in the lukewarm shallows.
Then the cow came down to the shore to lick the salt.
'Remember the swing of the tide?' she asked him, lowing.

But he could not. His nails curved only a little on her hide,
his eye teeth kept their usual places under his upper lip.
He felt used-up, outmoded, fogeyish, not latter-day...

The weight of the werewolf's hand on her backbone
increased the cow's depression, the drag on her hooves.
Morosely and without the moon, they waded together.

The Zone Begins

The Zone begins in a courtyard so deep with darkness
it is more a well than a convivial place where
washing's hung and the light at night from windows
braids and unbraids across the space, convivial too.

Not light, but a damp blackness reaching fathoms down
then leaking from that square to start the Zone.
A wooden bird hung from a balcony stirs in the air,
turning a half circle slowly and then turning back.

Ethnographers in moon suits will collect it one day
when the Zone's ticking weakens into breath, to pulse
of unseen trees, original stuff of birds like this
whose intricate wings and tail are one cut piece.

Until then it is drowning daily, nightly in the black
of this apparent cistern out of which springs the stream,
the Zone, all coal and oil and ebony drinking up
daylight, voices, shiver of branches about real birds.

Daughter of the Zone

A woman presses her grey cheek, her grey fingers
into the floor of the church in the Zone, as though
she would enter the ground below its chequered tiles.

She is old, as they all are who returned there
sometime after. The aged priest in the side chapel
moves from saint to saint, saluting their worn faces.

They are tarnished, filmed with damp; the juniper candles,
having staled from so long in the box, smell of
a subtle rot, the roof leaks a puddle past the woman.

All of them finite, sentenced: ten years or so and
it will all be over – only the dead in consecrated
ground, its congregation dwindled to thin air...

Even that Perdita, Persephone, the once-lost child,
with her face all points and the close-cropped skull,
may not last out the winter now the Zone's in her blood;

though they cosset her and keep her from the damp
of tiles and puddles, hustle her from gravestones,
away from the metal of the saints' cold haloes.

Oh daughter, who should be rolling in a field's spring flowers,
you are thin and white from keeping in the dark.
Your pupil is a black way back into the ground.

Atlantis

So, at the bottom of the vent in the sea
through which Atlantis disappeared, is
the Trojan horse like a discarded toy
all luminous with wet in the dark.

Achilles floats upward led by his buoyant heel,
a calm pale criss-cross in the turmoil,
as all that is underwater beats and bubbles,
voiding what first was swallowed.

Achilles Acted

Inside the narrow cell of light, he turns upon his heel.
The leather coat fans out, encompassing his striding
studied walk over the darkened stage, driving this light
before and all around him: Achilles, 'lion-sick',
pacing out upon the ground the dimensions of his cage.

And ours, who tune our breathing to his breath, whose eyes
tick to his measure to and fro within this closet box,
the doors of which are shut upon us all, 'And I myself
see not the bottom of it': Pandora's carton, crucible,
hope-chest, coffer for treasure, glass-fronted display case,

shut hand that can fan out in opening, almost fly
across the blank of light – to Troy, at least, and tents
of Greeks, the night sky of the seashore dense with stars
above their linen ceilings. We exhale as one and let
our elbows wrestle extra space along with 'rank Achilles'.

Then, on our legs of eyes, we leap down to the stage,
entering the stretched, extended air in the 'great Myrmidon's'
wake as he, 'the sinew and the forehand of our host',
drives on between the lines of lesser soldiers –
an army of them, two, ten years of war to trifle with

inside this toy box, play pen, theatre, bloodied world
where battle's smoke and red and wooden staves
and scimitars that clash and spark, light clenching
and unclenching to grasp the 'great and complete man'
within its fist again. Here Achilles 'keeps thicket'.

Looking for Helen

Posthumously, no doubt, she was for a while enshrined
as one of those archaic statues who step forward ever,
whose arms spring away from their sides and,
most mysteriously of all, who smile, just a little,
their lips tip-tilted, their eyes alight – all of them alike,
a family with exuberance just contained and going somewhere
out of the mirk of time, lit by their golden marble radiance.

It seems like grace, as if they had found a secret
that we lost later. The Gioconda's just-there smile
is far more earthly, explained by human speculation
as early pregnancy and so on. But these seem angels
from a sphere that's not our own. Their stone
is lantern thin, and a light inside it forever burning.
Helen was of this separate, this god-involved time.

And her statue rocked on its pedestal until it fell
crashing into the silent pool below, forcing a surge
with its sinking, then row after row of waves radiating
from that gulping spot, to decline at last to ripples –
the ripples that have not stopped. So she lies
on her underwater bank called by the names of Troy and Sparta,
at ease as she's shown in history, accepting this fate too.

                    *

Just after dusk in December,
the temperature has commenced its plummeting,
cold of the stone parapet strikes upward through my elbows
as I lean there to look down on the quantity of swans –
forty-plus and still arriving one by one in the mauvish dark.

Paler than the moored white packet boats,
paler than sheets of paper in my hands, they blotch the dock,
patterning the water with their equal separation
each one from all the others, moored boat shapes
rocking quietly on their own, sufficiently.

Behind me the rush hour pulses, underneath
the arches of the bridge the sparrows flock
and fiercely chatter. I am islanded between.
And some of the more-than-fifty swans below are sleeping,
heads pillowed in their wings on the icy water.

           *

But there's no escaping for all the time.
Someone cut off the wings of a cygnet in Bristol Docks.
Under the Trojan windows of the swan-derived Helen
men died in their blood in her name again and again.

The wondrous archaic smile is daubed from the sacrifice,
heat rising still from the entrails on the altar before it.
Kali, necklaced in skulls, red tongue hanging like a bib,
stands better for that side of her than talk of angels...

Which is in part my argument: the lady at the heart
of this long-known story remains as elusive as steam
when it rises and cleaves a moment to the mirror
then comes away on the hand as water simply.

The metaphors queue up to be applied to her, their transfer
darkens the dazzle of her white skin; but there they sit
upon the surface. All of those eyes that looked on Helen;
where is the "I" of Helen, the subjective she?

           *

Inside the eggshell the tiny girl babies stir
and make mouths at the pearl light
filtering in to them from all curves.

They must beat their way out of there beakless,
with down-soft palms and melting joints,
with naked gums and not-yet-welded foreheads;

but for the time being they only twine
and slide their twin flexible spines
against the white membraned lining of the Leda egg,

44

more birds than children, nested far
from their mother's heartbeat, laid on the ground
and warmed with cloth and grasses.

They must have looked later for feathers
sprouting at their joints, for the growth of webs
between their toes and fingers, for wings most of all;

how unfair to be born of a swan-god and a woman
and granted no gift of flight at all,
no chance to fall asleep on the water's glaze.

*

Clytemnestra, the twin, killed Agamemnon in his bath,
murdered Cassandra for accompanying him as booty
back from the sack of Troy. Her palms are directly bloody
and drip into the lustral basin, staining transparent water.
She struck in revenge for the death of her daughter
and died from revenge at her son's hand, her story ended.

But still explicable: one cause brings on effect
that in its turn transforms itself to cause; and Helen's sister
lifts her hand closed on the knife because she hates
the man who did her mortal hurt, striking the life
from her womb with casual sacrifice of her child
to meet a pack of raiders' need for Troyward wind.

So whom did Helen hate, whose death would she not forgive
and where did she give her heart? I cannot say...
It seems at the end of it all she returned to Sparta
and Menelaus's bed, the war an interlude wiped off
the chalkboard with an easy swipe of a wet rag:
wife still, queen still, still the revered living Venus.

Not even appropriate death neatens these events.
Philostratus and Pausanius present her afterlife
queening it on the Fortunate Isle with Achilles for new husband
and a great abundance of beasts both wild and tame.
In these tales they feast the characters of Homer,
measure verse with recollection over the wine cup passed.

*

Libations in the Spartan orchards
to Helen Dendritus, goddess of the trees.
On the red sandstone tombstone
in Prague's St Vitus's cathedral,
the foliate swan whose wings
turn into branches and then to leaves.

Divinity makes the difference.
The goddess walks on water
and switches at her own will
from swan to tree or Helen,
thus missing any consequence
of hurricanes sent against the city.

Thus missing the human too –
the need to find a way
out of the hole you're in
through cunning, generosity or something...
If you can change your coat completely,
why patch and darn old tears?

                    *

See Greta Garbo in the anonymous trenchcoat and slouch hat,
the perennial dark glasses, as she dodges photographers
into a dim-lit alley and away. See Marilyn Monroe,
sewn into flesh-coloured silk scaled with silver sequins
and lit by a haloing spotlight as she slowly and breathily
sings 'Happy Birthday, Mr President' to her lover, JFK.

Edward James designed and had constructed
a sofa to mimic the red lips of Mae West.
The potters of Greece, learning their craft from nowhere,
moulded the first-ever bowls from Helen's breasts –

which same, in their sudden nakedness, in the night sack
of burning Troy, caused Menelaus to drop the sword
he had sworn to use in murderous vengeance on her,
and take her back to Sparta on the same terms as before.

                    *

46

Freeze the frame.
Let the actress focus on that motivation:
she must decide – was this really a chance encounter
or did Helen see him coming from afar
and let the dress drop to her waist,
knowing the way he would react,
confident in her witchcraft?

Did the deaths below her windows
feed that power –
each one too much to be forgiven her
but still forgiven;
though they recognised her self as source of all their ills,
they laid down their lives
because she was palpable beauty?

And she felt that
and floated a little farther off beyond them
with each mourning wail
raised suddenly in the palace precincts,
feeling the swan wings budding at her back,
the water trodden down under her heels –
believing her own publicity, in fact?

                    *

Aphrodite was after all her agent, who promised Paris
'the most beautiful woman in the world' as a blackmail
to gain the golden apple Strife labelled 'for the fairest'.
This is the other aspect of god-involvement:
the plucking up and setting down again elsewhere
at a higher will and quite without consultation.

The pledge was given before Helen met the Trojan prince,
before the firebrand boy arrived at Menelaus's palace
on some mission to regain an aged aunt from the Greeks.
He knew what awaited him, strode inside with moistened lips,
but she may not have been readied for the stranger's claiming looks,
her ignorance and sense of safety meant to spice the pillage.

Most show her willingly stolen; there are nonetheless accounts
in which it was rape indeed, along with all the Spartan treasure.
And then the gods took sides throughout the resultant war,
Apollo against Athena, and the rest, prolonging the death tallies,
prolonging Helen's Asian detention – if that is what it was.
Even falling for Paris might feel ersatz once it had been ordained.

                    *

'No will, no will at all,
only the long drawing towards him
through all the labyrinths of Troy,
as though his bright hair were a magnet,
his muscled flanks.

I hear them call me whore
for my sleepwalking journey to him
with rapt face and fixed gaze,
ignoring others' greetings in the passages –
as I go to unbuckle Paris's breastplate.

Menelaus was an old man,
famously bandy-legged
and stringy-thighed.
His bed was a cold place
meant for wrestling.

But this one out of the East,
with scented armpits
and glorious oiled curls,
makes me sink then float again
when he comes in from the slaughter.'

                    *

'The marshes stink at my back,
these men with their plucked and oiled female bodies
stink before me. Asia, sink of the world
and my unwilling destiny, to be holed up in a palace
crowded to bursting with Priam's fifty sons,
while my countrymen are cut down at the door
and my realm rots ten years without me.

Sparta on its clean dry hill
with the clean dry wind driving through it
and the sound of sheep doing their peaceful usual things
coming to me from the distance...
At home they hang my image in the orchards
to stir the fruit towards harvest:
here I am whore with no function but the bed.

Aphrodite, I long to curse you
for bringing me into your private narrative.
When Paris was guest in the palace where I was queen
we owed him the hospitality we gave him
like any stranger arriving at our gate.
He is traitor to Menelaus, that good old man,
and traitor to me who brought him the welcoming wine flagon.

I wait for the alien walls
to be pulled down around me by my stubborn Greeks outside.
Blood reek within the citadel cheers me
and Priam's children wearing hack marks on their limbs...
Zeus, Father, make it happen soon – the consummation:
Troy down about my ears
and Paris in pieces at my feet.'

                    *

In fact, Paris was dead already when the wooden horse
was trundled in through a gap in the city wall.
And – perhaps the one scene that shows the "I" of Helen –
she patted the sun-warmed side, slid her fingers
along its well-planed belly, as it stood at last in Troy.

The gesture is ambiguous nonetheless, has the usual
at-least-two readings. One: that as Greek she understood
the subterfuge and plot going on, and that knock
with a flat hand was her endorsement – there being now
no doubt of her imprisonment, wed forcibly to Deiphobos.

Two (this I prefer): that here is Helen with, at last,
an inner life; that she liked the great brown creature
with its tucked-down head and scent of pine new worked,
fresh from the timber yard; that something about the beast
spoke a friendliness to her; this she acknowledged.

For the first time it is easy to see her circling round,
skirts bunched up in one hand, and a smile that turns in
to herself alone on her lifted face. She moves into the shadow
of the horse's mass then out again to the dazzle on the other side.
Queen Helen appraises the Trojan Horse as if she were going to buy it.

                  *

Not everybody buys this story anyway.
One tradition says that Helen never got to Troy,
that only her ghost passed along the walls for admiration,
only rumours of her presence fuelled the passions
that cut men down, kept them camped on the sands
for ten long years with only her faint scent wafting to them.

Either she was left in Egypt midway on the journey east,
or Sparta needed her presence so, that Sparta would dry up
without her – its rivers shrunk to needles in the sand,
its desperate sheep foraging among crumbling rocks,
its orchards barren with branches turned to claws –
the goddess held the land in the shade of her wing.

Which would at least explain her elusive character –
though it makes that war indeed a chessgame of the gods
in which every piece is just pawn to some degree,
and seems to deride the efforts of everyone concerned:
ripples slap the pond side quite at random
when the stone apparently thrown is a clot of empty air.

                  *

The dream again: stairs and stairs and stairs,
somewhere to get to on time but the steps
won't let me – they fetch up against blank ceilings
or turn transparent underneath my feet;
while the hands on the many clock faces
whirl like pirouetting skaters,
consuming a day as I lift the heavy hairbrush
in both hands.

This time it's a complex ruin I am navigating,
with centuries' strata in place of staircases
and congruence of walls that maybe indicate
this was the atrium, and maybe not.
The sun ticks too fast across the fierce sky
as usual.
I am looking and looking among the eroded blocks,
facing dead ends continually.

I ascend a slope of rubble
then climb down a cliff of columns to the ground.
The shadows are switched on like streetlights
and silk curtains drop down,
leaving only a little sandy path between.
Someone says 'Helen's here'
and I understand where I am going,
the fabric brushing my shoulders as I pass.

Usually in these dreams
I reach my destination a day or so late,
everyone else has left and my effort's wasted.
This time I find a figure at the end of the silken alley,
her white back turned...
When I circle I see the archaic smile again
and Helen in mid step
heading somewhere outside the frame.

She

No, not Lilith, copulating with sand demons,
dangling her talons above the strangled babies;
nor Mary the Virgin, a cradle for blood and bone,
whose hymen closed again after That Infant's birth;
but someone other, flying out from between
as a fleeting shadow, swift dim of the bright wall.

I need this figure that strides half obscured
as if by smoke; there's nothing for me in the
shopworn either-or of saint and whore,
hands tight or open; instead she must escape,
sliding where those others cannot go: underwater,
through the last light sliver at the shutting door,
into the maw of the whale and out again with
fistfuls of ambergris, past the sentries unseen...

She is the underside of the gunman's image
cast on the wall, the other shape the seabed perceives
when Ulysses passes above in his boat – a fluid,
uncertain-edged someone that could be anything...

IV

Marsyas in Hell

That shining skin that Titian pictured slung on his shoulder
in the red-flecked gloom, Marsyas, all sinew and
scarlet muscle, strides on his hooves over uneven ground.

He is the god down here, not that Apollo delicate
with the flensing knife, attentive to the gore that
welled from the satyr's flesh to greet his blade.

Serene in Hades: having chosen defiance of the deity
when he lifted the pan-pipes to his lips and won
the laurel from King Midas rewarded with asses' ears.

A petty revenge from a spoilt divinity, who might
pluck off the wings of dragonflies that offended,
who eased off the skin of a Marsyas hung by his heels.

And the third of them Harrowing Hell on Holy Saturday,
offered a rescue to the half-man doubly naked
where he stood in his blood and meat – to be refused.

It was a magnanimity not expected when he challenged
Apollo to display his music's best in competition,
an escape not then upon any probable horizon.

That was a Faustian compact and he knew what he was about –
impossible to beat a god, unthinkable to surpass
such superhuman skill, yet he was bound to try.

Goaded to unequal contest by the artist's impulse,
Marsyas cast it all into the ring, to be awarded
his own skin in a bolt that he unrolls and wears

as a shining cloak on holy days in Hades when
he strides as an Underworld immortal in the flames
that dry his bleeding, that proclaim the triumph of his act.

Penelope

History has me in this scene as the trapped fly;
someone's accomplished finger must poke in
from outside, sweeping away the sticky ropes
that bind me...
                    Really I am the spider, in control.
Twelve and one hundred princes wait in my web in parcels,
live and fresh and juicy should I choose one today.

I like this power.
                    The eight corners of the hangar-hall
in which my suitors hang about, are simply there
to hook my warps and wefts on.
                                    And see how I make
their anxious eyes follow my arm in graceful motion
driving the wooden shuttle through the silk and silk.
They wait for my words as though words were little cakes.

It's true that I am the cook, the baker; and until
I am through with the act, have bitten off the last
thread of my weaving, everything is potential, and
I sit inside creation like a cloud.
                                    Each shape is here,
every man; I scan all the profiles in princes.
It's riches, this tangle of random strands,
the dough set for rising, a mackerel sky...
I choose not to confine it, not to choose.

Portrait of a Lady

An Isabel Archer fails to affront her destiny
in the back carriage of a Tube train on the Circle Line.
In the space between the seats three youths are
vaguely gymnastic and speculate, when doors open
a yard short of the platform, on the meaning
of the yellow notice: 'Do not alight here.'

One points to the neon tube above him and jokily
says, 'That's a light'; but, deciding in the end
it's a warning against smoking, the translation
that they offer is: 'Do not light up here.' She doesn't,
she's dim in the brightness of the carriage,
lapsed and contemplative below the posturing boys.

Destiny is distance; but here and now, close at hand
is the journey in a circle she can turn continuously
through the whole day if she chooses, or perhaps
postponing choice, refusing a progression on the route
towards her fate spun in one of the three women's hands
where they stand, white-headed in the tunnel's dark.

She lags anyway – at the back of the parade of
neon carriages trundling forward. She got in there
deliberately, away from the bustle of the central cars
where all the strap-hangers appear to be on business,
to have a purpose, against her own abeyance... 'Do not alight'
unless you have decided, the yellow notice says repeatedly.

Drowning Out

1

Paperwork and water. They climb inexorably until past
the noses of those head down at the staffroom desks.
Registers drift by them, trailing threads of ink that
reassemble into ever-fainter ticks and zeros on the
burgeoning flood. Marks out of ten or twenty transfer
themselves to any surface – a resting naked forearm
or a windowpane, the sole of a tilted shoe – tattooing
blue-black the whole of Miss Augustine's regular dream...

She drowns. She sees herself float upward to bob against
the ceiling along with swollen textbooks and sodden
coursework files – equal detritus of the teaching process.
The building sags with water under, around and over
her. There's no escape into an afterlife of oxygen
or sunlight. Piece by piece in the soup she comes apart...
Then comes awake in sweated sheets with the morning
pressing grey against the windowglass, alarmed...

2

Turn your back – as so often to write upon the blackboard
in that simplified enlarged hand, while behind you
the classroom festers with shuffles and muttering and
you linger on the last smear of the e before turning
back to it all. It is just the same to set your face
into the anonymous air beyond the drowning building
and set off down the path away, away, such muttering
as tries to follow foiled by the shield of your back...

Don't look back, Eurydice. You can escape the shades
clustering the corridors in their repetitive clothes.
They were living once but now are dead to you, turned
to statistics on the blotchy page, turned away from
the give and take of class discussions, turned moody
and hollow-eyed as if exams had come for good and
all conversation were a disguised test to get them
into Elysium with its filtered sunlight, or black Hades.

3

She looks into strange lakes for the person she never
became. The waters offer alternative readings
of her tilted figure: Anne Augustine as a cloud,
Anne Augustine turning into rivers as her fingers
stream away into the general mass of wet then
shoulders sprout translucent wings a moment,
Anne Augustine almost a woman but quivering
at every edge like a washed dress in a wind.

She crouches to peer closer and sees her face grow
then disappear to give way to the stones and weed
of the lake bottom. Breath makes its own wind
and pleats the surface of the water – all that there is
of her until a hand slides forward to dabble
the shallows, making a shadow like a cloud
on the lit bed below... Begin with these fingers,
bereft of chalk stick or red-ink pen at last.

Anchoress

Here am I in my anchorite house with the grave
dug ready at my feet.
                        But only a virgin can catch
the unicorn in the oval of her mirror, lay down
its white head on her intact lap, strike tame
from untameable like the quickening of dead flint.

So the power broods in me within four walls
with just the squint to the altar as a space
to take my breath with it from here out to the forest,
where the pale creature slips between two tree trunks,
silent upon its toes.
                        I can have it as Christ figure
if I will; but have it I will anyway when I can –
the white beast at my beck outside the door
or at my heels, following as a lap-dog does
the scrape of my skirt-hem on the earth.

Capitals

1 *St Jerome*

Stone lion in a stone study,
leaning above a table strewn with books
to lose the thorn that pains its paw.

The saint strains across
from the capital's corner,
squinting at the beast's gigantic foot

that is the centre of the sculpture.
He forgets the hard stone
with which he beats his breast

to fend off carnal visions
from the surrounding sandy wilderness
that now engenders lion.

Lion with a bovine face
and the slender shanks of Arab horses,
the mane which is in part a patriarch's beard.

Never mind. Jerome has recognised it.
He has stopped his long study of the Hebrew
to attend to this stony task.

2 *St Eustace*

It would rather be liquid than stone,
this story, this image.
The wind blew, the boughs of the forest bent.

His dogs ran ahead of him
as he followed the tireless stag
till dusk and through into the darkness.

His horse and he flagged
underneath the unseen branches,
though the chase continued.

All this precedes the seminal encounter,
the moment of conversion,
the crossing of the bridge

between before and after,
when Eustace brings his horn up to his lips
and the stag turns, lifting

among its antlers the cross of light
from which the impassioned voice demands
'Why persecutest thou me?'

The best that the stone can do
is freeze the frame right now
as the cast of figures unclose their mouths.

3 *St Vincent*

What poses with more patience
than one of God's own dead?
St Vincent in repose

lies where he is deposited
with folded hands,
martyred in a soft feather mattress

that precluded any further torture
on the grid-iron of saw blades
laced with stinging salt.

But this corpse
that shows so passive
is animate in its own way.

Cast into the sea in a bag
weighted down by a millstone,
it nevertheless inexorably swims ashore...

Here the eagles that watch his body
to keep wild beasts at bay
may be pinning the nude limbs down...

Perhaps only this suit of stone
holds him anchored in the church
who might otherwise float through the wilderness at will.

Air Writing

Mount Ararat is an extinct volcano erupting only air
into the Armenian blue as blind Noah begins his
"masterpiece" at the table attended by daughters.

They fuss and bib him, count the pages out against
the fingers of his left hand, curl his right about
the pen and clink its nib upon the china inkwell.

Extinct Mount Ararat made no protest when the Ark
engraved its summit with a weighty keel like
a stylus pressing down into the pinkish tufa.

Now air scrawls invisibly on its surface, and Noah
initiates his last great work, dipping the pen nib
then shaking it a little before it's applied to paper.

The plain sheets to the left are covered with writing
then moved to a pile on the right. He works into
the night day after day, making a molehill of pages.

Remaking a mountain in his head perhaps – that
peak reappearing underneath his boat as the waters
fall, slopes asserting themselves again in open air.

So he writes and reaches the end and dies at the table.
And the paper is shuffled back into a useful quire
since his daughters have withheld all ink from him.

The old make messes of themselves, they thought,
and black is the devil to wash out of clothing;
he's blind and need not know about his thwarted dream.

What was written with air on the unstained pages
and breathed up on the air from criss-crossed fibres
like the fume of heat off Ararat on a summer's day?

What essence of water, what long immersion now
condenses upon the walls and ceiling of this room
where Noah confided his final wisdom to the pen?

God's conversation fails to erupt for posterity's awe,
the death of almost all creation fails to materialise
from the extinct volcano of old Noah's paper hill.